The Quarrelsome Computer Keyboard

and other poems for Children

Barbara May Boot

Published by New Generation Publishing in 2015

First Edition

www.newgeneration-publishing.com

Dedicated to my Grandson James, and my grandaughter Emily

Contents

Tractor Terror.

The boy watched the farmer
While using his plough.
He thought! that looks easy
I'm sure that I'd know how.

While the farmer was having his lunch,
The boy on the plough did jump.
He pushed a lever to make it start,
It lurched forward with a bump.

Down the field the tractor sped,
But the boy did not know how to steer.
He started to shout for the farmers help,
But the deaf farmer could not hear.

The frightened boy tried his best
To make the tractor stop.
But it trundled on towards the hedge
Then flung the boy on top.

Sandcastles.

A boy on a beach a sandcastle built,
With walls that would last forever.
Three turrets and a deep, deep moat,
It would never fall , no, not never.

But no one told the boy on the beach
About the incoming tide.
As the waves came nearer and nearer
The young boy watched with pride.

But sooner or later it had got to happen.
The waves the castle had reached.
And in a very, very short time,
The castle walls where breached.

The boy could not believe his eyes,
As he watched his castle tumble.
He thought the walls would last forever
But the sea had made it crumble.

Puddle Walking.

A boy walked by a puddle,
It didn't look too wide.
So be tried to jump over it
But couldn't reach the other side.

He landed in the middle,
Got wet up to his waist.
His trousers got so very wet,
He ran home in great haste.

He explained to his mother,
The puddle was not very wide.
But he could not jump over it,
To reach the other side.

The Christening.

My baby sister is christened today,
But I don't really care.
All this fuss getting dressed up
I would rather go quite bare.

Mom says I cannot wear
My favourite spaceman's suit
Or even my cowboy clothes
With spurs upon the boot.

I must be clean and tidy
On this special event.
And wear a shirt with a tie,
I think I'll hide in my tent.

By the Muddy River.

The day was sunny and bright,
But the boys where very unhappy.
“Lets go to the river” one boy suggests
Where the waters all dark and muddy.

They ran down to the river bank,
Throwing their socks and shoes off.
And stared with great surprise
To see a stranded whale with a cough.

“I’m stranded” said the whale,
“Oh please can you help me”
“Where do you want to go” they asked.
“To the open sea “ said he.

So they waded into the river
And pushed with all their might,
Till the whale was free from the mud
And then swam away from sight.

The boys looked at other
Then clapped their hands with glee.
They hope the friendly whale
Managed to reach the sea.

The Broken Swing.

Two children ran into the park,
Intent on having a slide.
But the slide was wet and cold,
So on the swings they did ride.

They swung their legs very fast,
Making the swings shiver and shake.
In fact they swung so very high,
The nuts and bolts began to break.

Now the swings where broken
They went down the slide so bold,
But when they reach the bottom
Their pants where wet and cold.

Making Cakes.

"Can we make some cakes today"
Molly asked her mother.
"No not today" her mother replied.
"Go and ask your brother".

"Can we make some cakes today"
Molly asked her brother.
"No not today" her brother replied
"Go and ask your mother.

I've asked my mother and my brother
To help me make some cakes.
I'll ask my dad he's sure to help,
Just as soon as he awakes.

Boys on a Cycle.

Two young boys on cycles where racing
Round the park and by the lake.
Two old ladies on a bench where sitting,
"Don't go so fast for goodness sake.

The two boys carried on regardless,
Whirling round, and round the trees,
Taking not a bit of notice,
Of the old ladies taking their ease.

Once more round the lake they went,
Going faster and faster still.
Then they stopped, looked at each other
Both agreed they felt quite ill.

A Robot and Two Boys.

A robot walked along the street,
His arms and legs a-clanging,
A beacon light upon his head,
Red, blue, and green lights flashing.

Two boys came riding along that street,
Happy and loudly shouting,
Full of fun with not a care,
Their legs happily swinging.

Then they saw the robot,
With beacon lights a flashing.
They stood and stared with great surprise,
At his arms and legs a-clashing.

But the robot took no notice
Of the two boys on bikes riding.
He just ambled down the street
His arms and legs a clanking.

Toys On a Bed.

There is a line of furry friends,
Sitting on my bed.
They chit and chat all day long,
Not a cross word is ever said.

The rabbit is a light brown,
With two long furry ears.
He has a smile upon his face,
He's been on my bed for years.

Another little furry friend
Is a lamb, white and woolly.
Wearing a pale white jumper,
He looks quite sweet and funny.

Then there are two teddy bears,
One brown, holding a baby.
The other wears corduroy pants,
A check shirt that is trendy.

Now this line of furry friends,
Are happy and serene.
To sit upon my bed all day,
All smiling and very clean.

The School Cricket Team.

My junior school has
A very good cricket team.
We play in the springtime,
It is good to let off steam.

We practise in the nets,
With bat and cricket ball.
Billy is our captain,
Because he is quite tall.

We play our matches on Sundays
Against our local schools.
Eleven players on each side,
That is the golden rule.

Billy is the first to bat,
He hit a mighty four.
The next ball hit his finger,
And made it very sore.

After that poor Billie's finger
Began to puff and swell.
He was in a lot of pain,
The look on his face to tell.

When Billie's finger was examined
It proved to be badly broken,
He could not play again this year
So our side was very weaken.

So without poor Billy
We did not win a game,
As the cricket season ended,
We held our heads in shame.

Better luck next year!!!!!!!

The Donkey Ride.

It was a lovely day by the sea,
So a donkey ride I did go.
Sitting up on the donkeys back,
Gently swaying to and fro.

Other children where having rides,
Up and down the beach.
From one flag in the sand
Then turn, the other flag to reach.

My donkey and I where happy
As along the beach we did plod.
His sturdy feet taking each step.
As over the wet sand he trod.

Then all of a sudden it happened,
The donkey stopped in his track.
He held his head up to the sky,
And gently arched his back.

I tried my best to coax him
To carry on with my ride,
He dug his toes into the sand,
He would not take a stride.

Now all this time the
Tide was slowly coming in.
I told the donkey we would drown,
But he just gave me a grin.

Then as the water reach his toes,
He suddenly started to run
Back up the beach where we started
It really was quite fun.

Scarecrow and Friends.

The scarecrow stands tall and straight,
In a field of growing corn.
With a sad look upon his face,
Feeling alone and quite forlorn.

His head is a squashed round turnip,
His jacket full of holes.
A pair of old wellington boots
That keep pinching all his toes.

He guards the farmers corn field,
From all the thieving crows
As the corn begins to ripen,
In rows, and rows, and rows.

A little robin has made a nest,
Inside the scarecrows coat.
Also by the wellington boots,
Theres a home built by a stoat.

The stoat and little robin,
Are very friendly indeed.
They keep the scarecrow happy,
With all his daily need.

My Friend Harry.

I have a very special friend,
Who comes and plays with me.
We jump and run, along the beach,
And paddle in the sea.

Sometimes we just sit and watch
The boats go sailing by.
Harry and me are very best mates,
We are never ever shy.

We take a picnic to the beach,
Nice sandwiches and cakes.
Perhaps some biscuits and pop,
And bread my mother bakes.

There is a park near where we live,
Where Harry and I sometimes go.
We take a ball and little hoop
Playing catch to and fro.

Now you might think Harry
Is a little child like me.
But you would be mistaken,
Just you wait and see.

For Harry has four furry feet,
Can jump just like a frog.
He is my very special friend,
A very, very, cuddly dog.

My Baby Sister.

Our home is a happy place,
With mom and dad and me.
We have some lovely parties,
When gran comes round for tea.

Then one day mom came home
With a little bundle, small
I looked inside and saw a face
All pink like a soft round ball.

Mum said "this is your little sister
Who is going to live with us".
She started crying and kicking her legs
Because she didn't like all the fuss.

I didn't like her crying,
So I tickled her little feet.
She stopped, and looked at me
It really was a treat.

She is too small to play with me
As she sleeps quite a lot.
All snuggled in her blanket,
In her new white baby cot.

When she is a bit bigger,
She will play with me.
But until then I will be content,
By letting her sit on my knee.

Washing Day.

Washing day is here again,
Lets hope the weather is fine.
Then the washing can have a blow,
As we hang it on the line.

The towels swing with gusto,
The vests and panties to.
The socks are in their pairs
Dancing two by two.

The nightie and pyjamas
Get tangled in the tree.
Then a gust of wind comes along,
And quickly sets them free.

The pretty little dresses,
Are hanging so serene.
They are the cutest flower frocks
That you have ever seen.

When the wind blows the washing,
It's like dancing to and fro.
The flapping of the woolly socks
All hanging in a row.

The Three 'Ps

The potato started down the hill,
The pizza tried to follow.
The pudding said "I'll catch you up"
But they forgot the stream was shallow.

The potato was the first to arrive,
The pizza caught up quickly.
The pudding kept getting stuck,
Because the grass was prickly.

The potato jumped across the stream,
The pizza did a gambol.
The pudding was out of breath,
He fell straight into a hole.

The potato found he was in a field,
The pizza was wet and dirty.
The pudding got out of the hole
And tried to do a curtsy.

The potato looked, and saw a cow,
The pizza started shaking.
The pudding did a little quiver
At the noise the cow was making.

Cows have quite a good appetite,
So he ate the potato, pizza and pud.
He felt quite queasy when he had finished
So he sat down with a thud.

The School Sports Day.

The children where all excited,
School sports day had arrived.
The sun was shining in the sky,
The teachers where revived.

Excited little children,
Where put into their groups.
According to their size and age
With skipping ropes and hoops.

The first race was a running race,
The children sorted in size.
They ran their little legs off,
Eager to win first prize.

The skipping race was next,
Children lined up with glee.
The whistle blew, they where off,
Legs all tangled up, trying to get free.

The next race was the hoops,
Girls and boys standing ready.
Feeling very eager to go,
While holding their hoops steady.

The relay was the last race.
Everyone had a turn.
All lined up together,
The teams extra points to earn.

The day had been a happy one,
With the sun up in the sky.
The children running races,
Wishing they could really fly.

The Swimming Lesson.

The swimming lesson was going well,
All the children excited.
Learning to swim with armbands on,
Very happy and delighted.

One child under the water did go,
They shouted "he will drown"
"O no he won't" the coach replied,
As he watched him with a frown.

The little fellow tried to reach
The side of the swimming pool.
The coach just stood and watched him,
Feeling some what like a fool.

Then he suddenly realised
The child could not get out,
So he ran to the side of the pool,
And pulled him out with a shout.

The coach was not very pleased
With this unruly little boy.
"I was only looking for fishes" said he,
Looking all sheepish and rather coy.

Swinging.

A little girl on a swing did sit,
Swinging high into the sky.
Laughing our loud with mouth wide open,
She didn't know she had swallowed a fly.

The fly, it landed in her tum,
As the swing swung slower and slower.
It didn't like the damp and dark,
So out it flew on to a flower.

All this time the girl was happy,
Swinging high up in the sky.
Laughing so loud, quite contented
She didn't know she had swallowed a fly.

My Pretty Knitted Jumper.

My nan knitted me a jumper,
With a pretty scene on it.
The sleeves where long and cuddly,
It was a very good fit.

On the scene was depicted,
Animals of all shapes and sizes.
From rabbits, horses even cats,
It even won lots of prizes.

The background was blue and green,
With some clouds and trees all leafy.
The animals standing in the grass,
The sheep all white and fleecy.

When I wear this pretty jumper,
I get admiring glances.
At the animals standing there,
As the horse and rabbit prances.

Then it happened I grew to big,
The jumper was too small.
So I put it on a hanger
And hung it on the wall.

The colours are still delightful,
The animals quiet and serene.
I am sure it's the prettiest jumper
I have ever seen.

My Favourite Place To Be

I have a favourite place
At the bottom of our garden.
Where trees and bracken grow,
And a bench that is wooden.

This is my secret hiding place,
When I am feeling sad.
A place where I can be alone,
Till it makes me quite glad.

This special place is very quiet,
Where I can read my book.
Or just sit and let my thoughts
Wander, like a babbling brook.

Sometimes when I am feeling bold,
I imagine I'm a charging knight,
Sitting on my horses back
Holding on with all my might.

Sitting on the wooden bench,
I imagine I'm on a ship.
Sailing on the tossing seas,
On an adventure trip.

This is a magical place
Under the willow trees.
Where my thoughts can wander
Any way they please.

The School Football Match

The School Football Match.
It was the final match
Of the school football league,
The boys ready to have fun
Especially their captain Bill Greig.

The football game was in full swing
When the home team scored,
"It was a foul" the ref did cry
"That goal, it was a fraud"

The boys who were playing
Stood around in shock,
They raised their fists as if to fight
A raging battle did mock.

The referee took control,
He let the winning goal stand.
It meant the home team had won,
So the locals played their band.

The opposition were furious,
"That goal should not be counted "
They shout with rage, stamp their feet
Until their coach they mounted.

The Cup and Saucer.

The cup said to the saucer
"Will you come with me
I have been invited
To a very nice house for tea"

The cup and saucer looking very trim,
Set out along the road.
Feeling happy and serene,
And extremely bold.

When they reached the house,
Where they are having tea,
They met a very pretty plate,
Just as pretty as could be.

"You look very pretty"
the cup said to the plate.
"We are going in here for tea
so we must not be to late"

"Can I come with you" the plate asked
"Because you look just like me
We can all sit together
When we have our special tea"

The pattern on the cup and saucer
Where the same as on the plate.
So they made a happy trio
Passing through the garden gate.

My New Skateboard.

My dad gave me a skateboard
For my birthday just last week,
Its red, green, black and blue
With a shiny white streak.

It as two wheels in the middle
That go round quite fast.
You stand upon it very straight,
Hoping your strength will last.

My dad said be careful
When going down the hill,
Because it is very steep,
But really, it was a thrill.

At the bottom was a curve
I had not seen before,
But my skateboard did not turn,
So I crashed into a door.

I fell into the garden,
Then looked at the big scratch
My crash into the door had made,
Perhaps it will need a patch.

I picked up my battered skateboard,
And trundled up the hill,
It made me feel unhappy, in fact!
It made me feel quite ill.

My Sisters Wedding.

I am going to be a page-boy,
At my sisters wedding.
But I am a boy aged eight
It's a thing that I am dreading.

All dressed up in fancy clothes
A jacket with a flower,
But I could wear my anorak
If we only had a shower.

The wedding was to last all day,
Gave me a very big problem
I could not leave my pet Joey
He would cause a bedlam.

The problem I quickly solved,
I could put him in my jacket,
He would be safe in there
And not cause any racket.

When the service was over
A meal we where going to share,
I put my hand in my pocket
But Joey was not there.

I heard my auntie Nelly scream
"A mouse, a mouse is there
eating icing on the wedding cake"
I could only stand and stare.

I held poor Joey in my hand
Until the fuss subsided,
Then the bride and groom
On the dance floor glided.

My little pet forgotten
As people began to dance,
I just held Joey in my hand
And sat there in a trance.

Painting the Shed.

I was helping dad
To paint the garden shed,
We wanted it to look nice and clean,
So we painted it bright red.

We where wearing our old clothes
Old shoes and gloves as well,
But the paint splashed our clothes
And we began to smell.

The smell of paint was very strong,
As on our clothes it dried,
We could not remove it
No matter how we tried.

When mother saw us
She slowly shook her head,
"I thought you where going to
paint the garden shed".

We looked down at our clothes
They where smeared in paint,
We laughed and laughed at the sight,
But the shed it looked quite quaint.

Mud Pies.

Sitting in the garden
With the sun up in the sky,
It was so very peaceful
With the birds just flying by.

I watched my sister Mandy
Playing in the sand,
She was making mud pies,
With a bucket in her hand.

I closed my eyes then heard a noise,
I thought I must be dreaming,
Then I realised it was Mandy
In the sand pit screaming.

Her pretty dress was covered
With streaks of wet brown sand,
The bucket filled to the top
Had broken in her hand.

I ran to help the little girl
Who by now was crying,
But I could not remove the mud,
So I gave up trying.

I sat back down on the grass.
And tried to enjoy the sun,
But Mandy crying was so loud
It was hardly worth the fun.

The Quarrelsome Computer Keyboard.

The F and G where having a quarrel
Which letter held the record
About who was the most used letter
On the computer keyboard.

The A and S joined in as well
Then J and K followed suit,
All the letters where shouting loud,
But the E looked rather cute.

The numbers just sat and listened
To the dreadful din
All the letters where making,
It sent them in a spin.

The numbers tried to stop the noise
Saying we are used also,
But the letters hushed then up
And told them where to go.

"I am the most used letter"
said the jolly E
and skipped around the keyboard
as happy as could be.

The E calmed the letters down
Then started to explain,
"we all have our uses
so there is no need to complain.

"We have to work together
throughout the words we spell
to make them sound correctly"
the big fat E did tell.

The letters started to calm down
And then they all agree,
That E was right we need each other,
Then they danced around with glee.

Our Visit to Uncles Farm.

Mum took my sister and me,
To visit our uncles farm.
She said it was very old,
All rustic and with charm.

The day was warm when we arrived
So my uncle we went to find.
He was in the milking shed
With cows of every kind.

“Ive nearly finished” he said to us
“then I will show you around”
We waited in the cow shed
With mud all on the ground.

We got fed up of waiting
So my sister and me went to explore.
But the ground was very muddy,
We cleaned our shoes with some straw.

We found some sheep in a field,
Looking sleepy and docile,
So we chased them round a bit
But they where not very agile.

In another field we found
A herd of woolly goats,
The ones with horns chased us
So we just took off our coats.

The goats tossed them in the air
Getting them muddy and dirty,
We ran to pick them up
But the goats looked very shirty.

Mum was very cross with us,
When she saw our dirty coats.
We tried to say it was not our fault
It was the pesky, woolly goats.

Granddads Allotment.

My granddad has an allotment
Where he grows his flowers,
They really look quite pretty,
Thanks to the sun and showers.

He gave me a patch of soil
So I could have a go
To grow some lovely flowers
All standing in a row.

I sprinkled seeds upon the ground,
Then covered them with soil,
I was very careful
The garden not to spoil.

Granddad said to me one day
"If your flowers bloom and grow
are sturdy and up straight
we'll take them to the local show.

My flowers grew sturdy and straight,
With my loving care.
The patch of soil bright with colour
Petals, dancing the air.

We took some of our flowers,
To the next local show,
We put them in pretty vases
All standing in a row.

The judges came to view them
I could hardly believe my eyes
When they came and spoke to me
And said Id won first prize.

Granddad was very proud
And patted me on my back,
"Good work there my boy
you really have the knack".

My Old Rocking Horse.

I have an old rocking horse
That once belonged to my dad,
Some of his mane is missing,
He is looking rather sad.

I sit upon his back
Rocking gently to and fro,
In my imagination ,
Over the fields we go.

Sometimes when I sit upon him
I like to make believe
He is a famous racing horse,
His winning to achieve.

I ride my rocking horse
While wearing my cowboy suit
Galloping across the prairie
With spurs upon my boot.

His saddle is rather dirty,
Paint peeling off his head,
But I love my rocking horse
I think Ill call him Fred.

The horse is only made of wood
But very real to me,
When I sit upon his back
I like to rock with glee.

A Summer Holiday.

We are going on holiday
To stay right by the sea,
In a lovely caravan
Mum, dad, Tom and me.

We put the cases in the car,
Buckets, spades and cricket bat
Paddling shoes and lots of food,
Swimming costumes and a hat.

It seemed to take us ages
To the place that we where going.
We arrived at last, found the beach,
A ball we started throwing.

The ball it landed in the sea
We ran in to retrieve it,
But our clothes got very wet.
So on the beach we had to sit.

When mum and dad found us,
We where sitting on the beach,
We told them we where very wet
Because the ball we could not reach.

"Never mind" our mother said
"Just run about and play
you can be more careful
when we come another day"

The Visit From a Pigeon.

Sitting in the garden shed
My brother Alfie and me,
Chatting away about this and that
Enjoying a mug of tea.

A pigeon landed on the roof
Making a dreadful noise,
Flapping his wings and shrieking
It frightened us two boys.

All of a sudden it went quiet,
The flapping and shrieking stopped,
We opened the door to have a look
And inside the pigeon hopped.

The pigeon looked us up and down
Then saw our mugs of tea,
He flapped his wings and had a drink
Then landed on my knee.

We just stared at this lovely bird
Hopping about in our shed
Looking happy and content,
We left it and went to bed.

He wasn't there the next day
So he must have flown away,
Perhaps he will come again
To have tea another day.

The Castle Ruins.

Bobby, Jamie, Ann and me
Where going for a walk,
When we found a ruined castle
So quiet we dare not talk.

The walls, old and crumbling,
A tower tall and high,
The roof had gone completely
You could see up to the sky.

The ruins felt rather eerie
As we looked around,
With stones and broken rocks
All scattered on the ground.

"I wonder who lived here"
said Jamie to us all
"Perhaps a baron and his knights
where they had a stately ball"

They stood there in the silence
Afraid to even speak
Because they heard a strange noise,
Their legs going rather weak.

They did not like this ghostly sound,
It certainly was not fun,
They looked at each other, let out a scream
And from the castle did run.

My Horse, Toby and Me

I have a horse named Toby,
Who I like to ride,
Sitting on his sturdy back
Fills my heart with pride.

We gallop over the meadows,
With the wind upon our backs.
Then by the little babbling stream,
Following the trodden tracks.

My horse is usually placid
Very calm and quite serene,
Then one day it happened
He looked at me so mean.

We were riding by the farm,
I was holding the reins quite slack,
He came to a sudden stop
I slipped right off his back.

I went round to face him
He had a glint in his eye,
I could not scold my lovely horse
No matter how I try.

So I patted his long nose,
And tickled both his ears,
I saw the love in his eyes,
It filled my eyes with tears.

The Rowing Boat Ride.

Three boys in a rowing boat
Where cruising down a stream.
Enjoying the peace and quiet,
It was like a heavenly dream.

The little boat bobbed up and down,
As over the waves it glided.
But the water was getting deeper,
The boat, it nearly subsided.

The boys where laughing very load,
They did not hear the roar
That was echoing up the stream,
Like a very angry boar.

Suddenly they heard it!
The couldn't believe their ears,
It was the roar of rapids,
The boys, very nearly in tears.

They tried in vain to turn the boat,
But alas it was to late,
As over the rapids it did bounce,
At a very, very fast rate.

The boys where quite frightened,
Holding on very tight.
But they just bounced along,
Until they were out of sight.

A Trip to the Zoo.

Our dad took my brother Harry and me
On a day trip to the zoo.
We where quite excited at the
Animals we where going to view.

First on our list where the lions
With manes bushy and gold,
But they where all fast asleep,
Because they looked so old.

The monkeys where more exciting,
Swinging from tree to tree,
They looked cute and cuddly
I thought I would let them free.

I tried to open a little gate,
Where the monkeys ran amok
But it was shut with a bolt
And a very sturdy lock.

My dad saw what I tried to do
And was very cross with me.
"You cannot let the monkeys out
so lets go home for tea"

We travelled home in silence
after our trip to the zoo.
It was a pity really, so many
animals we did not view.

The Bear in the Park.

Freddy the knitted bear,
Sat on a bench in the park.
Hoping someone would take him home
But he was still there in the dark.

The children had gone home for tea,
They did not want the bear
Dressed in a woolly jumper,
They did not really care.

Freddy felt so lonely,
Sitting there all night,
Then a little fox spotted him
Just as it was getting light.

"You look unhappy" said the fox
to the bear who looked quite sad,
"you can come home with me
and met my mum and dad"

So Freddy followed the fox
to meet his mum and dad,
he was feeling happier now
In fact, he felt quite glad.

The Sleigh Ride Disaster.

It had snowed heavily
During the winter night.
The fields and hills covered in snow,
It was such a pretty sight.

When the three friends saw it
Joey, Sam and Billy
"Lets have a sleigh ride" Sam said
"and go where it is hilly"

They pulled the sleigh up to
the top of a near by hill.
Then upon the sleigh they sat
To enjoy the snowy thrill.

Several times they went up the hill
And then came sliding down,
But by now the slippery slope
Was getting rather brown.

"Lets have one last go"
Billy said to his friends.
But the snow being solid ice
Had created several bends.

The sleigh went faster, and faster,
We cannot stop they shouted
There are no brakes or steering wheel,
So a snowy hedge they mounted.

The boys all tumbled in a heap,
Looking quite pale and grey,
Then looked in horror at the sight
Of the broken, damaged, sleigh.

www.ingramcontent.com/pod-product-compliance
Ingram Content Group UK Ltd.
Pitfield, Milton Keynes, MK11 3LW, UK
UKHW020416250726
13967UKWH00007B/2666